DISNEY MOVIE FAVORITES

CONTENTS

This book is designed to be used with the following instrumental solo books:

00849922	Flute
00849923	Clarinet
00849924	Alto Saxophone
00849925	Trumpet
00849926	Trombone

ISBN 978-0-7935-3356-6

© THE WALT DISNEY COMPANY

HAL•LEONARD®
CORPORATION

7777 W. BLUEMOUND RD. P.O. BOX 13819 MILWAUKEE, WI 53213

KISS THE GIRL

(From Walt Disney's "THE LITTLE MERMAID")

Lyrics by HOWARD ASHMAN
Music by ALAN MENKEN

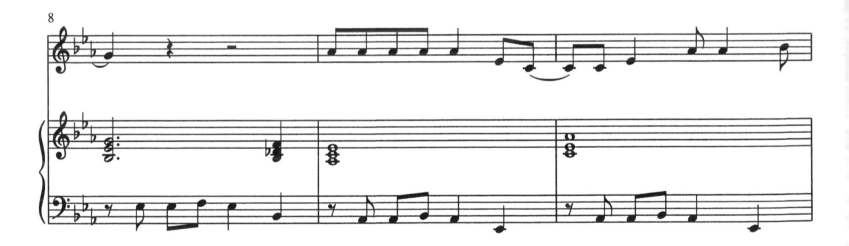

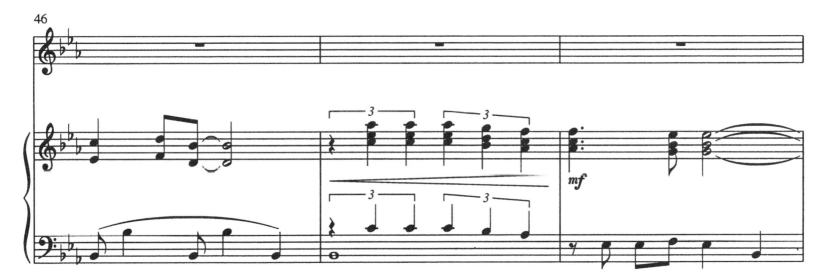

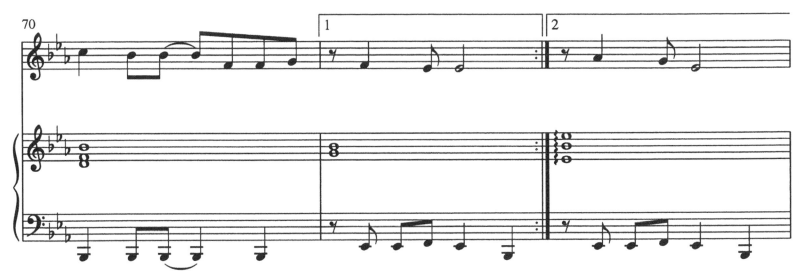

PART OF YOUR WORLD

(From Walt Disney's "THE LITTLE MERMAID")

Lyrics by HOWARD ASHMAN
Music by ALAN MENKEN

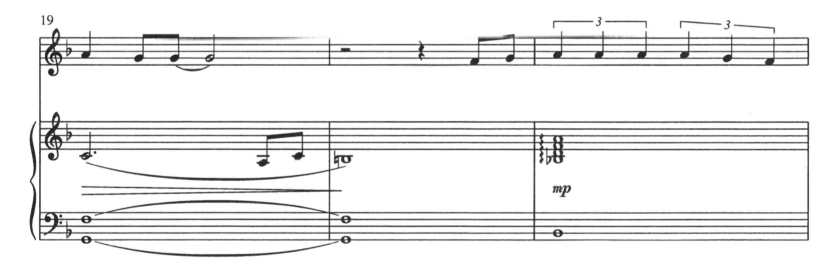

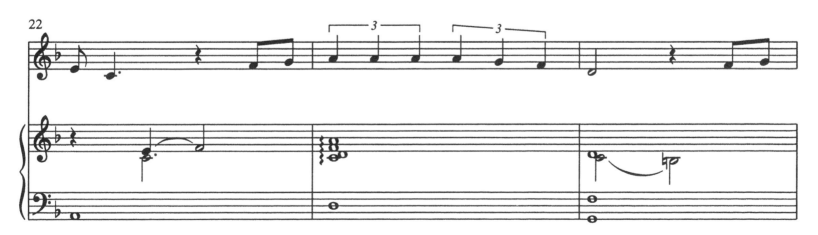

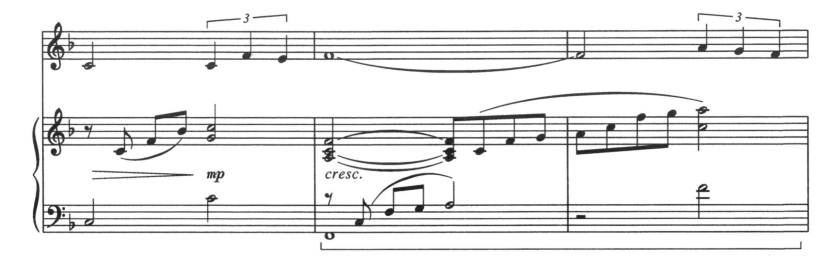

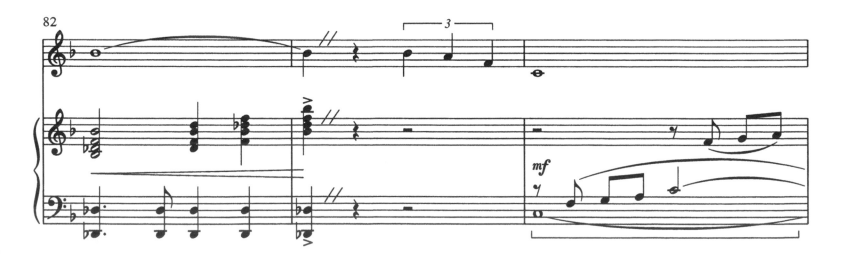

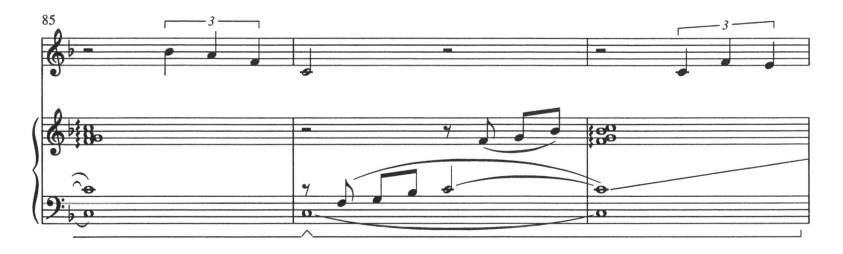

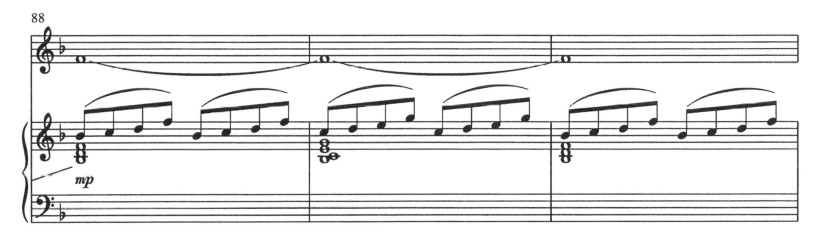

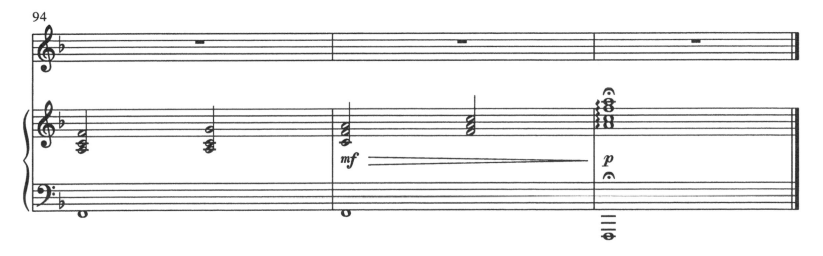

UNDER THE SEA
(From Walt Disney's "THE LITTLE MERMAID")

Lyrics by HOWARD ASHMAN
Music by ALAN MENKEN

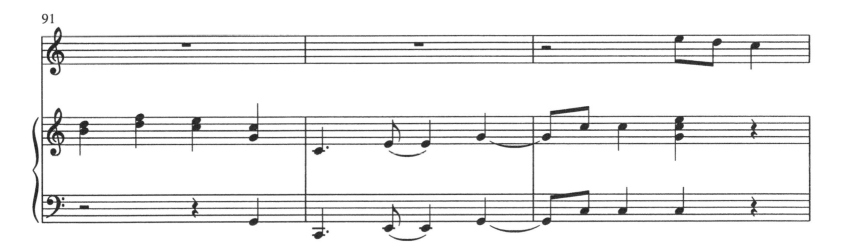

DAUGHTERS OF TRITON
(From Walt Disney's "THE LITTLE MERMAID")

Lyrics by HOWARD ASHMAN
Music by ALAN MENKEN

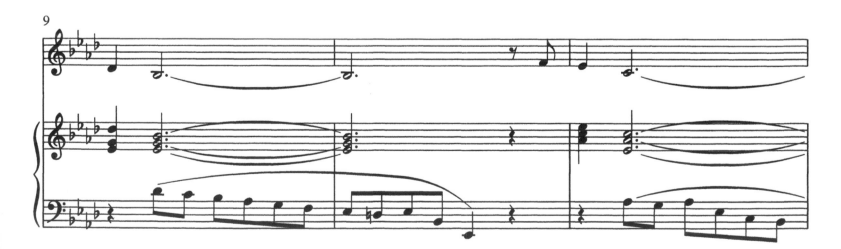

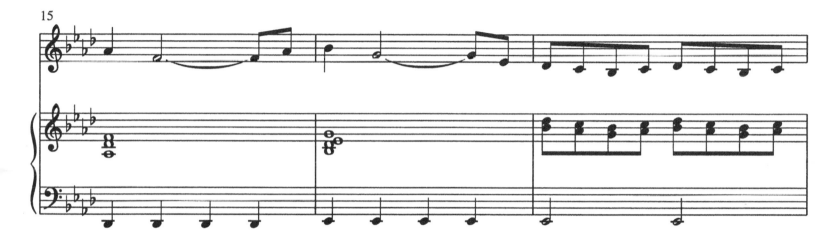

BE OUR GUEST
(From Walt Disney's "BEAUTY AND THE BEAST")

Lyrics by HOWARD ASHMAN
Music by ALAN MENKEN

Moderate tempo

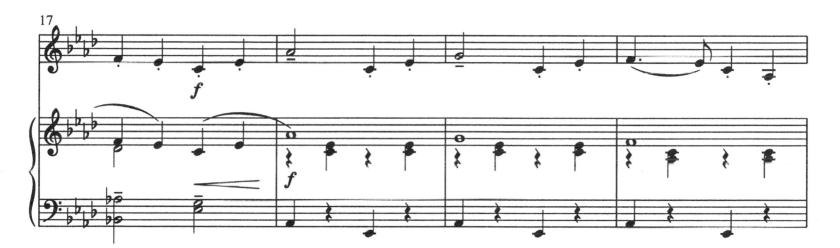

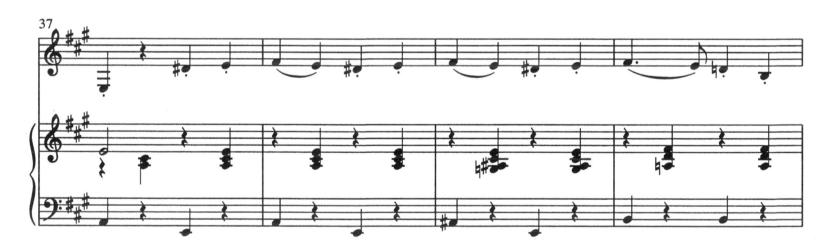

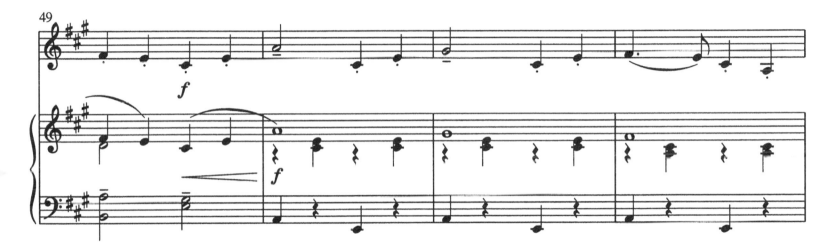

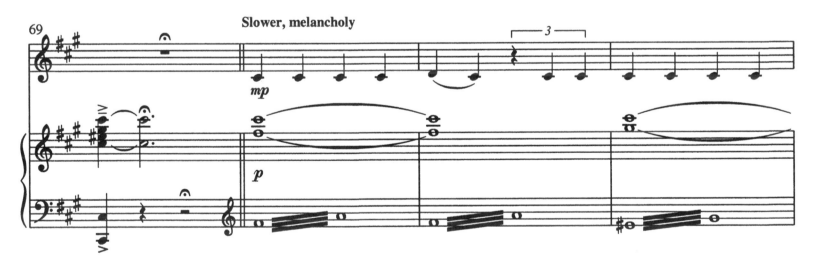

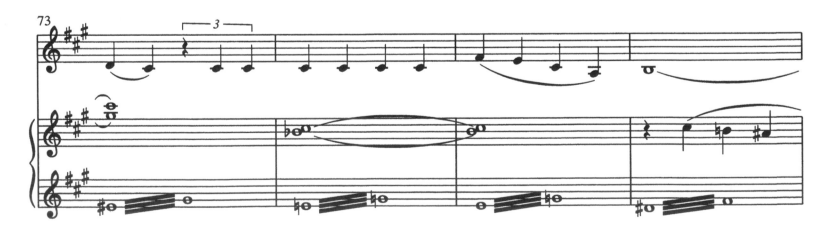

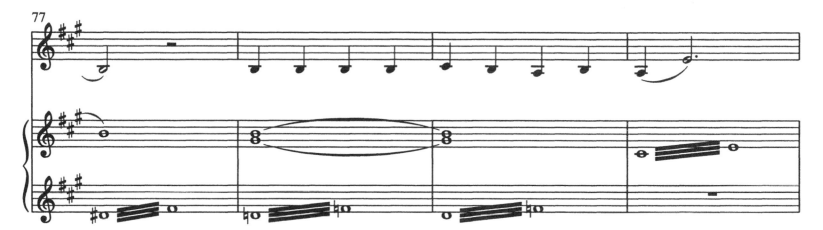

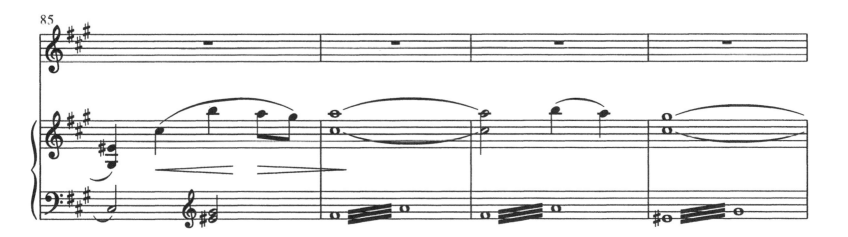

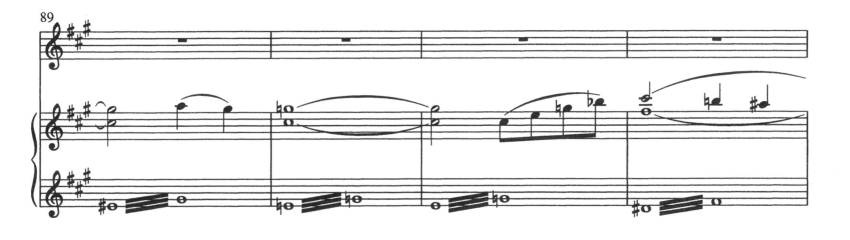

93

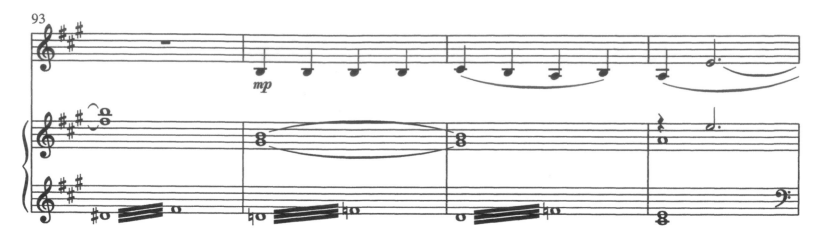

97

A tempo

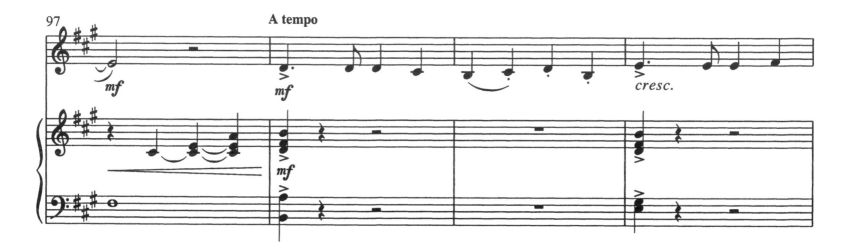

101

105

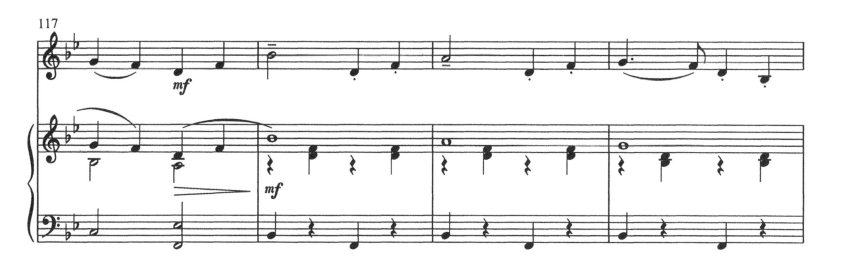

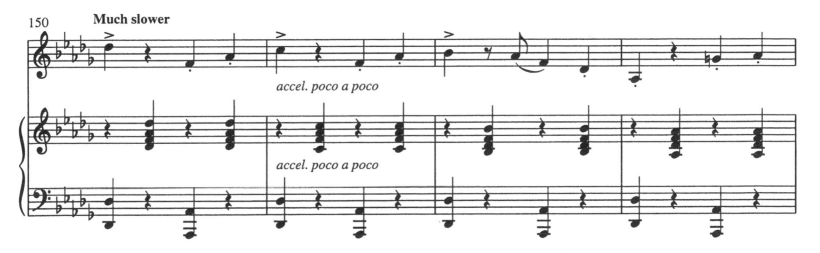

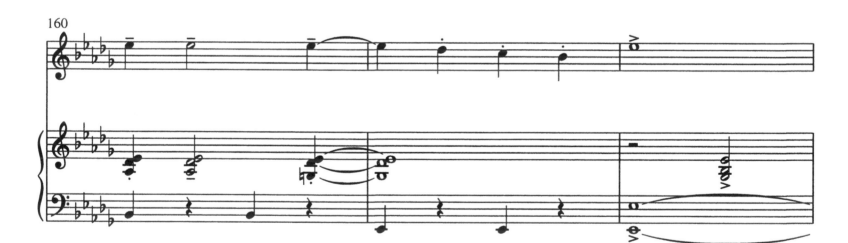

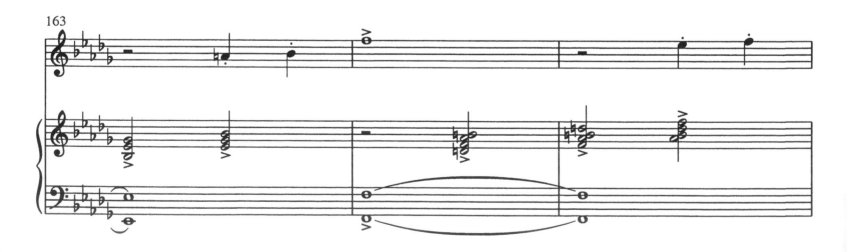

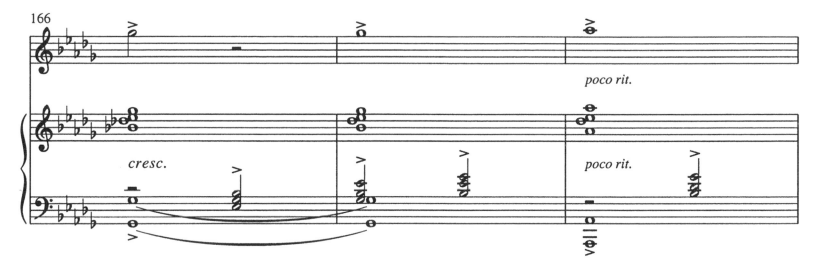

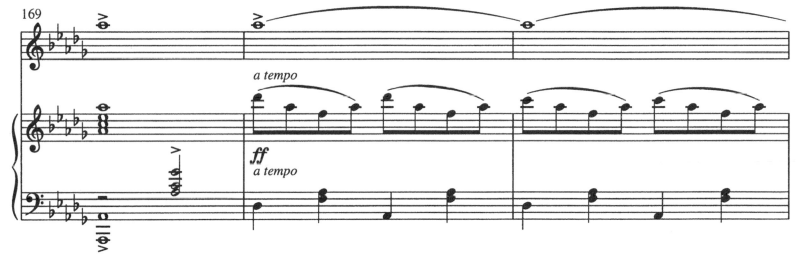

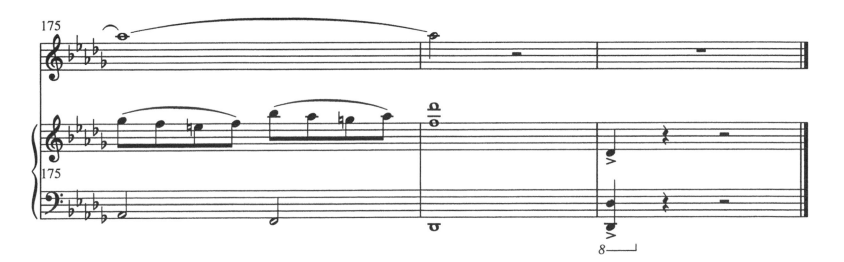

BELLE
(From Walt Disney's "BEAUTY AND THE BEAST")

Lyrics by HOWARD ASHMAN
Music by ALAN MENKEN

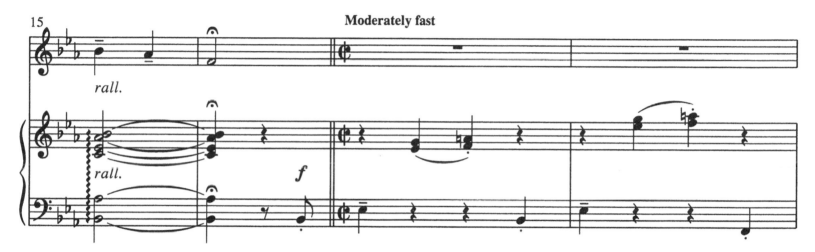

To Coda I ⊕

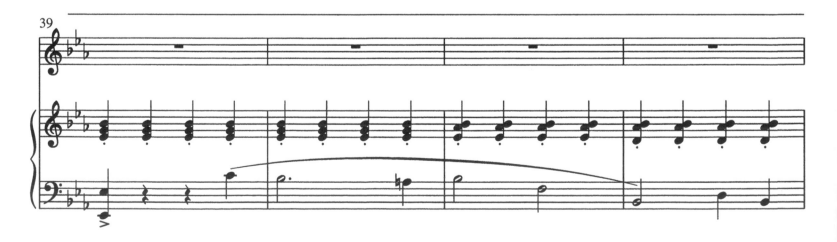

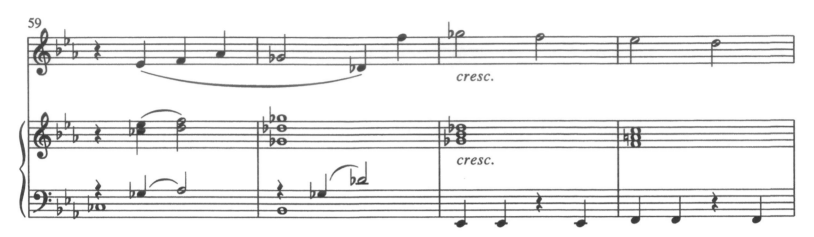

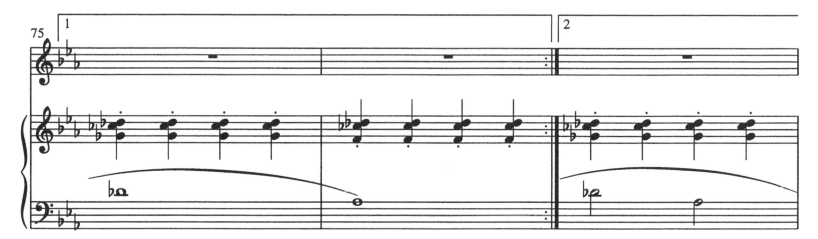

D.S. al Coda I

✠ CODA I

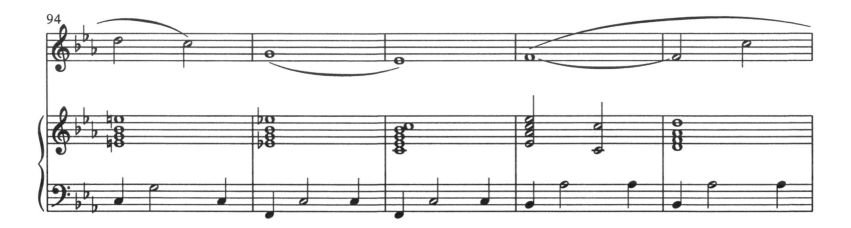

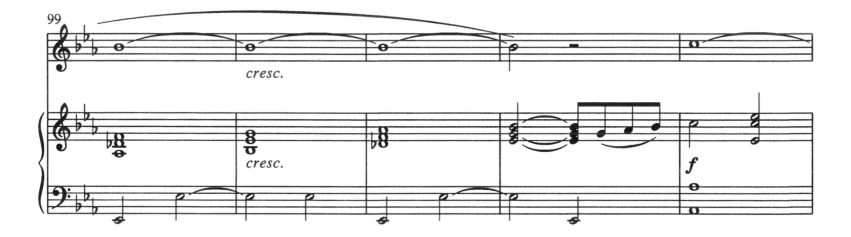

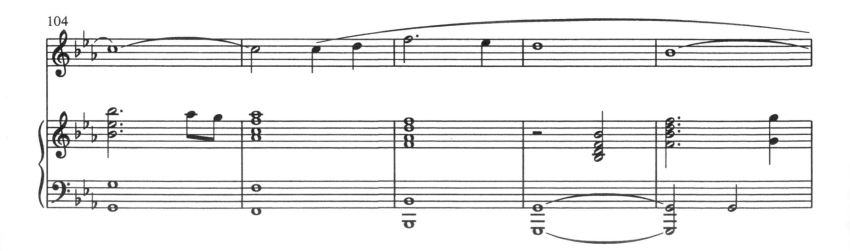

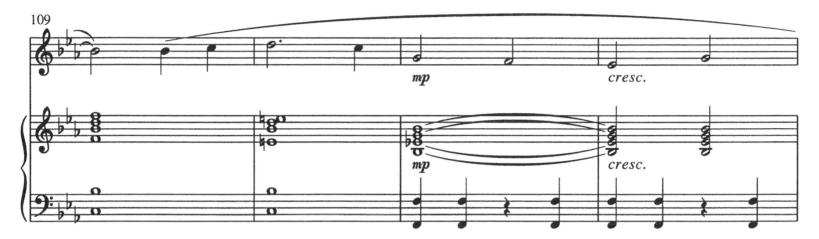

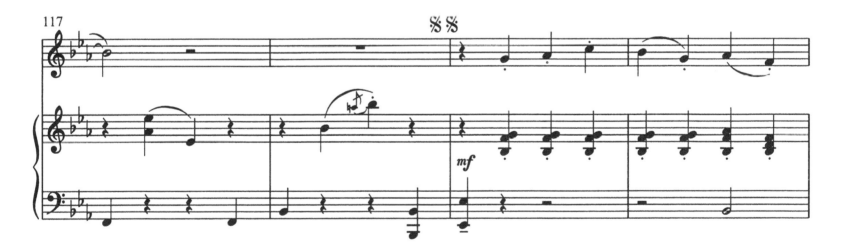

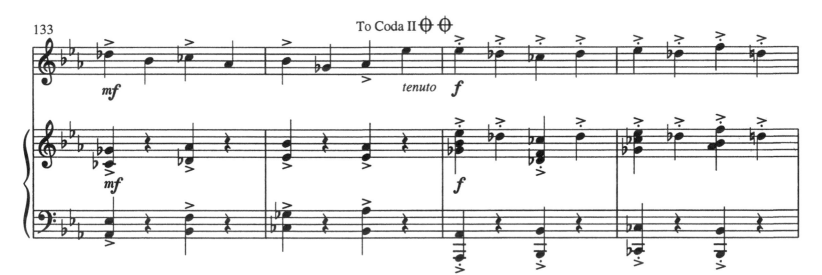

Pompously

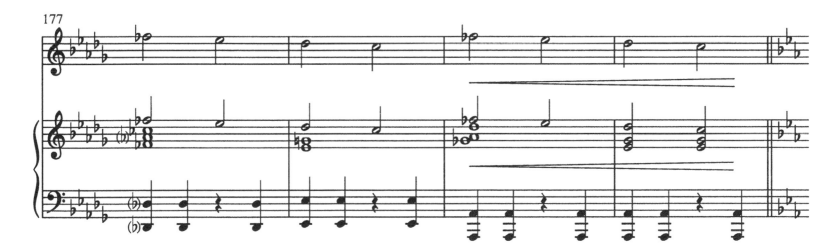

184

187

190

193

CODA II

GASTON
(From Walt Disney's "BEAUTY AND THE BEAST")

Lyrics by HOWARD ASHMAN
Music by ALAN MENKEN

Bright Waltz

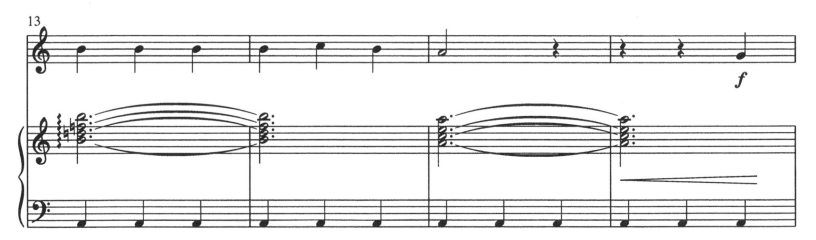

29

Barroom Waltz (played in one)

33
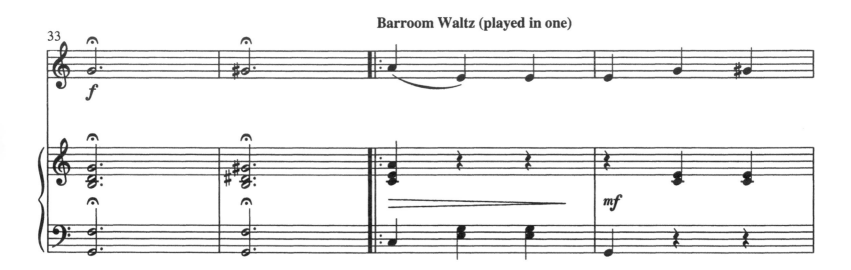

37

41

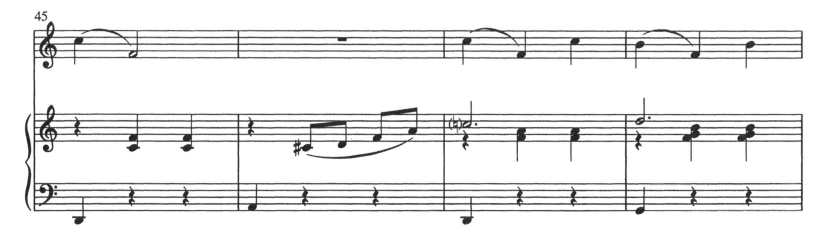

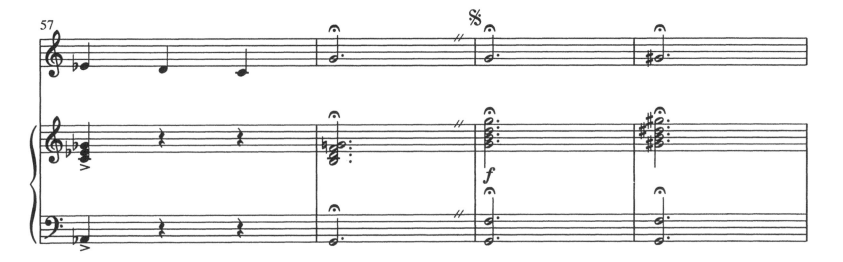

58

To Coda ⊕

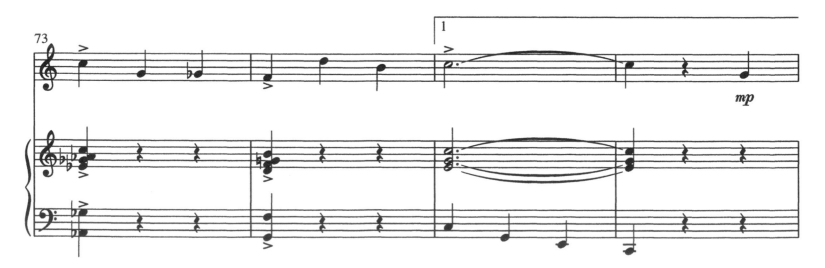

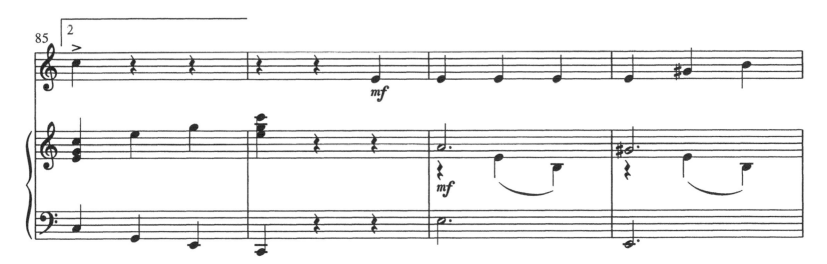

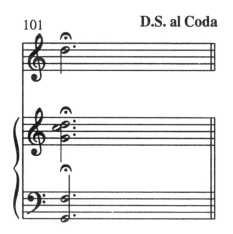

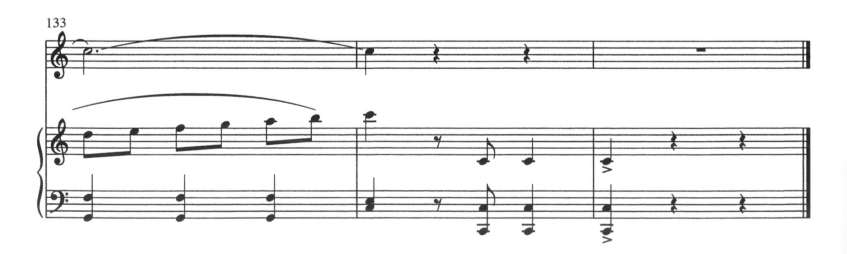

SOMETHING THERE
(From Walt Disney's "BEAUTY AND THE BEAST")

Lyrics by HOWARD ASHMAN
Music by ALAN MENKEN

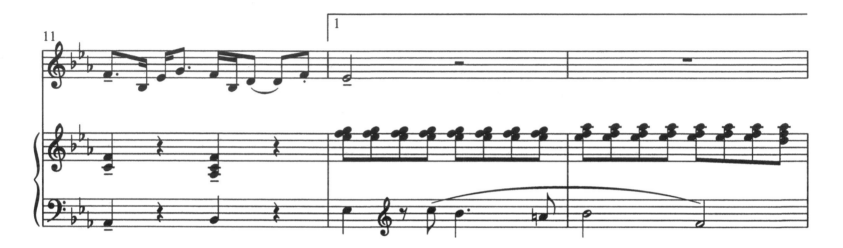

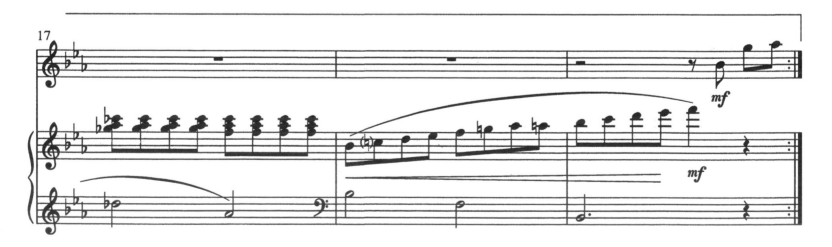

THE MOB SONG
(From Walt Disney's "BEAUTY AND THE BEAST")

Lyrics by HOWARD ASHMAN
Music by ALAN MENKEN

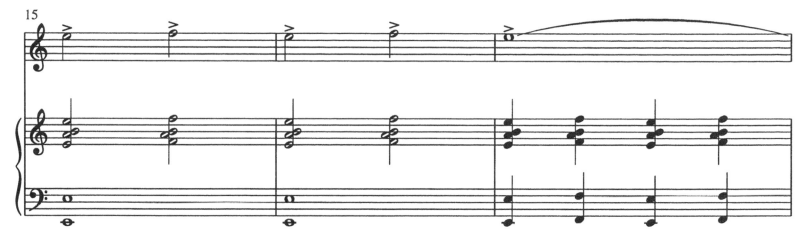

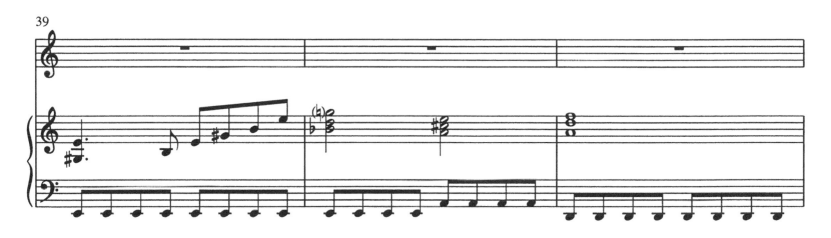

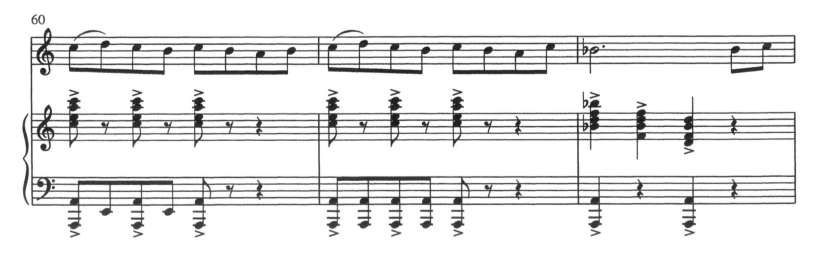

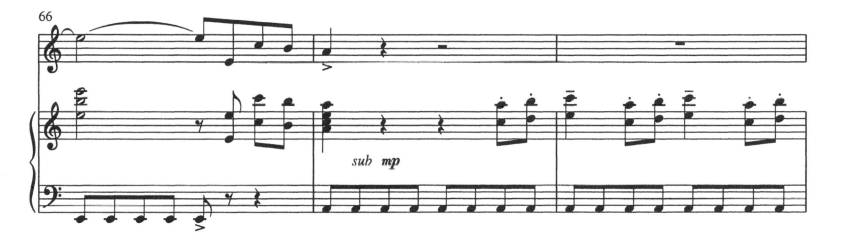

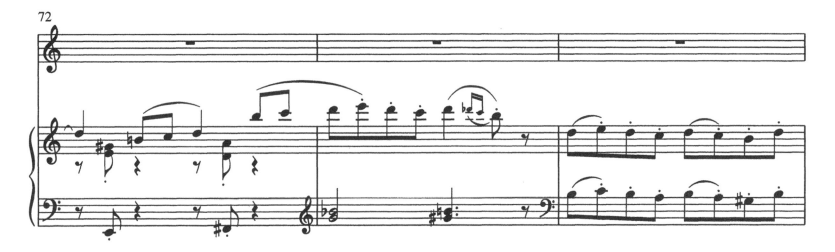

BEAUTY AND THE BEAST

(From Walt Disney's "BEAUTY AND THE BEAST")

Lyrics by HOWARD ASHMAN
Music by ALAN MENKEN

Lyrically

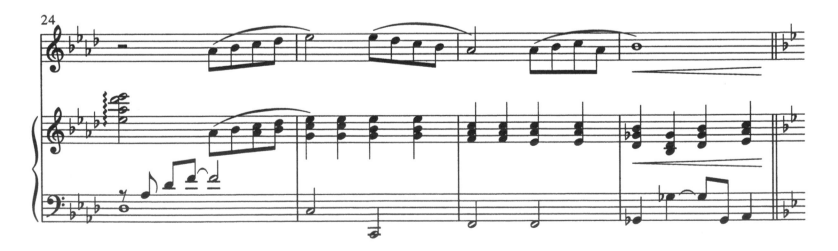

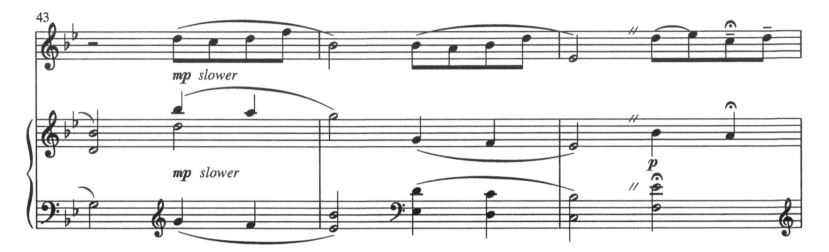

FRIEND LIKE ME
(From Walt Disney's "ALADDIN")

Lyrics by HOWARD ASHMAN
Music by ALAN MENKEN

84

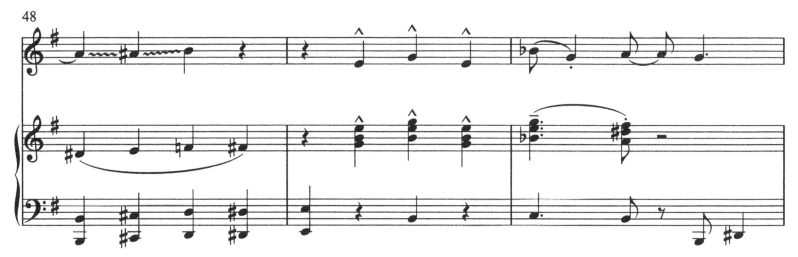

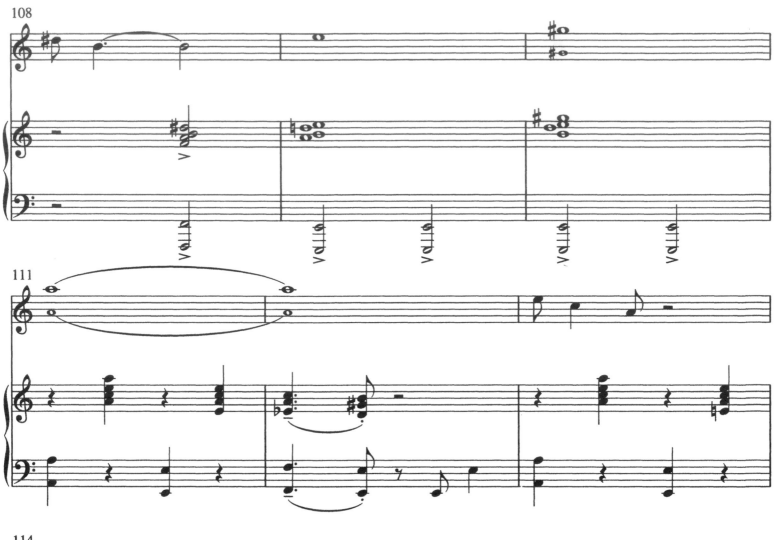

ONE JUMP AHEAD
(From Walt Disney's "ALADDIN")

Music by ALAN MENKEN
Lyrics by TIM RICE

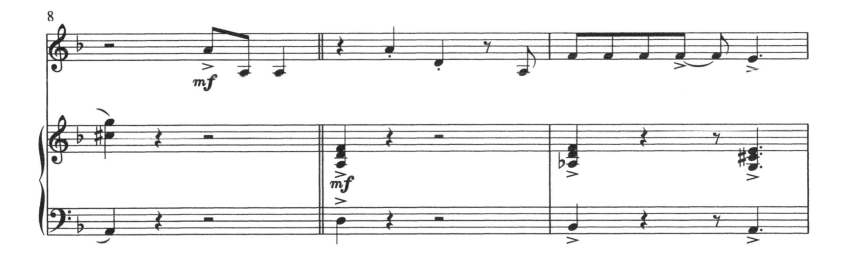

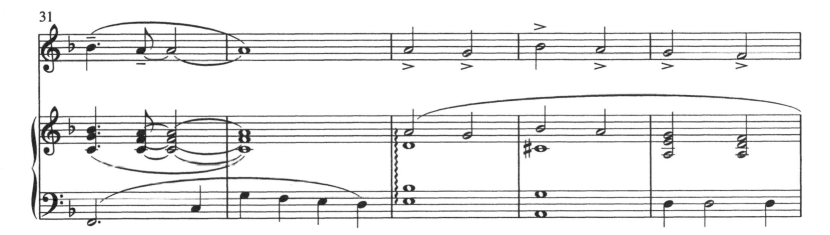

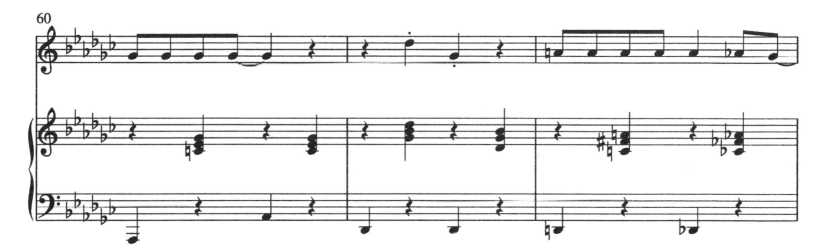

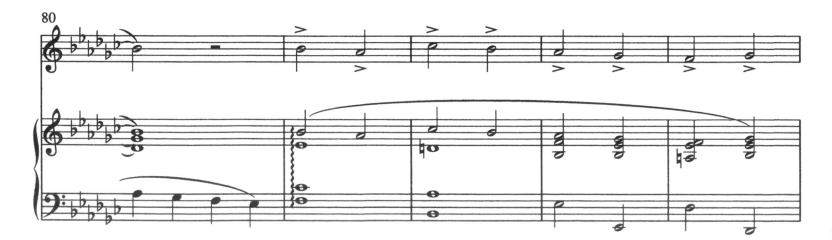

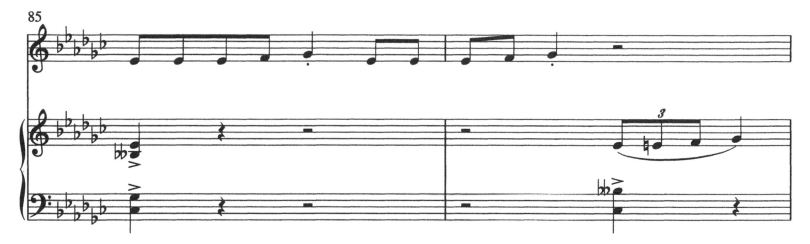

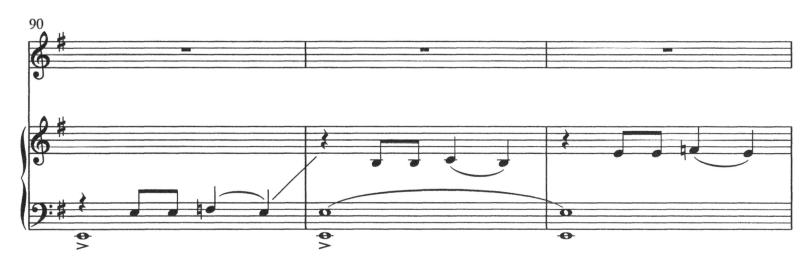

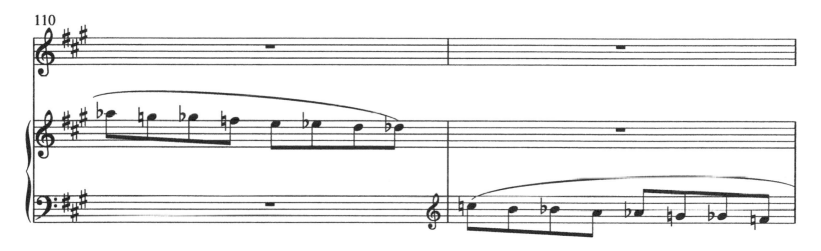

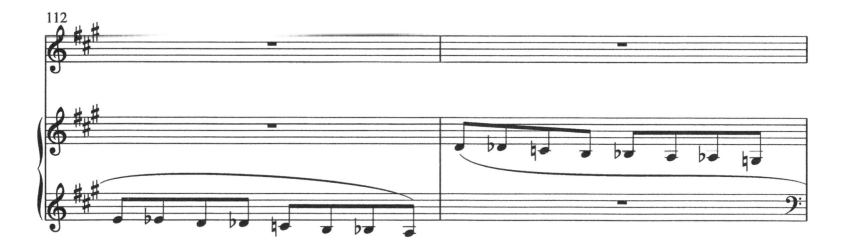

PRINCE ALI
(From Walt Disney's "ALADDIN")

Lyrics by HOWARD ASHMAN
Music by ALAN MENKEN

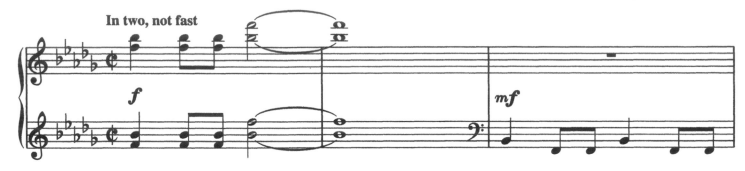

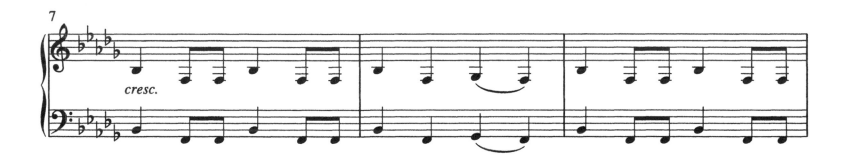

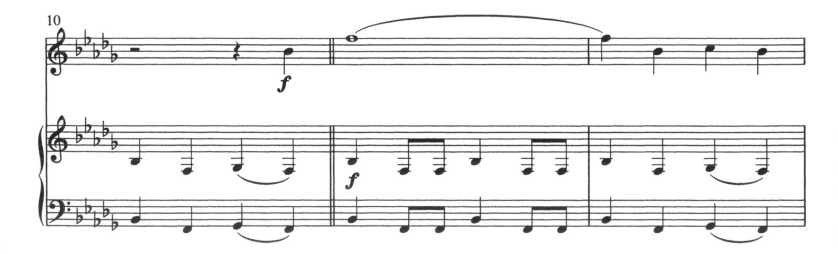

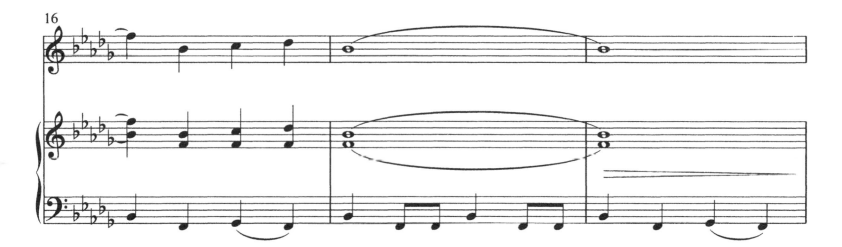

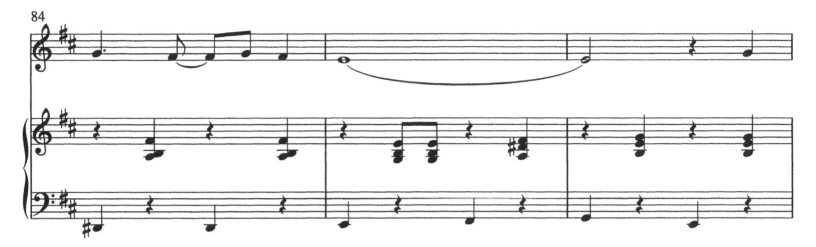

96

99

102

105

Tempo I

A WHOLE NEW WORLD

(From Walt Disney's "ALADDIN")

Music by ALAN MENKEN
Lyrics by TIM RICE

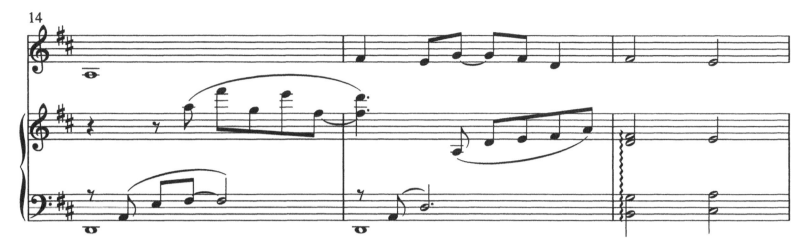

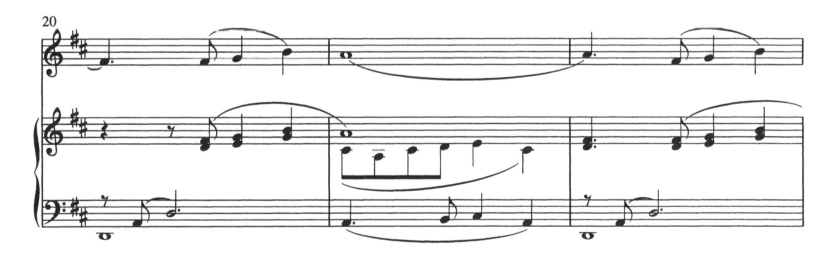

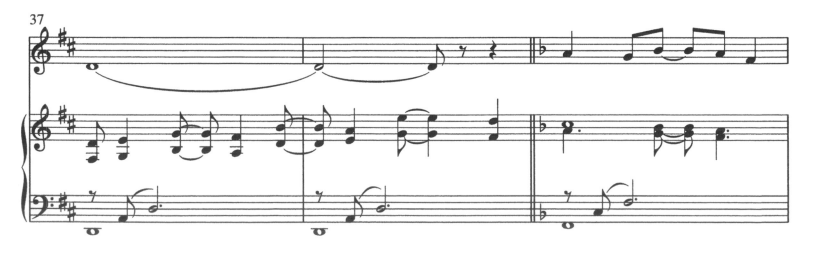

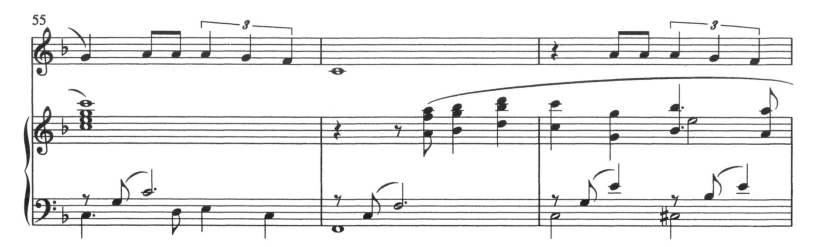

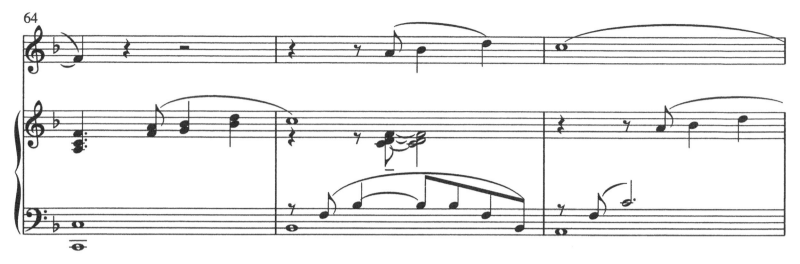

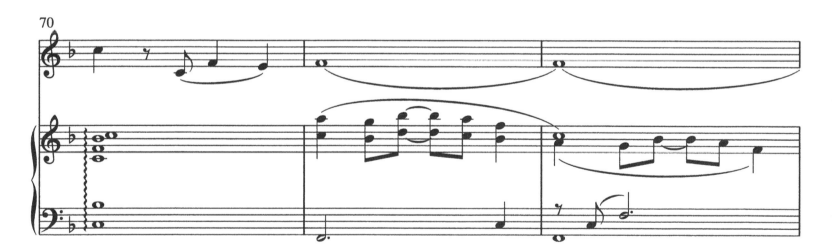

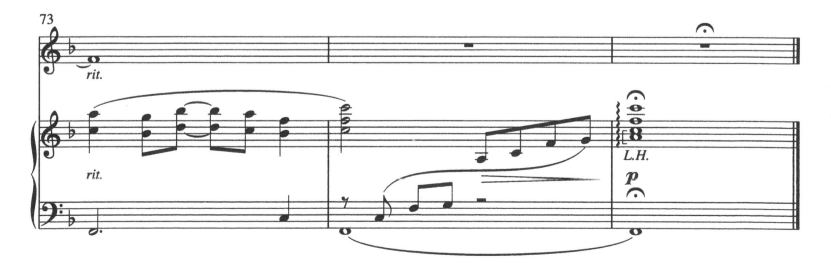

ARABIAN NIGHTS
(From Walt Disney's "ALADDIN")

Lyrics by HOWARD ASHMAN
Music by ALAN MENKEN

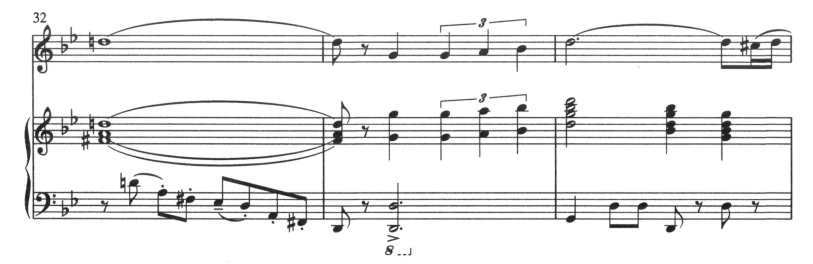

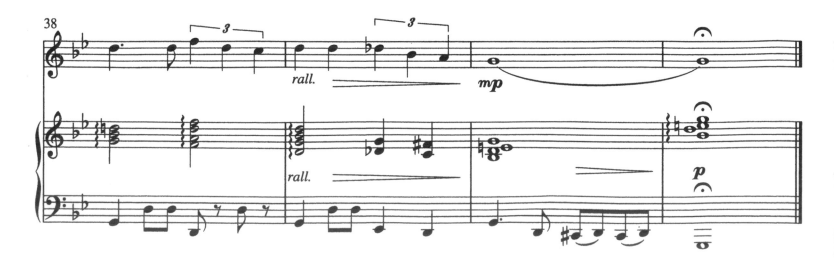